MCQs
On
Forensic Medicine

ARCHANA SINGH

Forensic Medicine

Copyright © 2020 Archana Singh

All rights reserved.

ISBN: 9798560500924

MCQs on Forensic Medicine

First Edition: 2020

© Publisher

Whole book or any part of this book may not be reproduced or modified or transmitted in any form, such as recording, photocopying or copying by any other platform of any type of system whether it is electronic or in offline medium without permission of author of this book.

ISBN: 979-85-60500-92-4

Price: 1000/-

US $: $13.33

Disclaimer

The author and editor have tried best to provide every information which is true to their knowledge related to the subject. Although author and editor ensure the optimum accuracy of the information and made every effort to retain the right information, yet it may be possible that some errors might have left.

The publisher, the printer, the author and the editor will not be held responsible for any error or inaccuracies.

Forensic Medicine

Description

The "MCQs on Forensic Medicine" provides access to the questions which have been asked and can be asked in upcoming examinations, such as, NET/JRF, FACT, or other exams in which these subjects are in demand. It consist 500 MCQs on Forensic Medicine.

This book consists of 500 MCQs of relevant to the Forensic Medicine. This book will help you to qualify NET/JRF examination as well as other competitive examination related to Forensic Medicine.

Edited By *@forensicfield*

Contact us:
Contactforensicscience@gmail.com
https://forensicfield.blog/
https://forensicfield.blogspot.com/
https://www.youtube.com/c/ForensicField/
https://www.facebook.com/forensicfield/
https://twitter.com/ForensicField
https://www.instagram.com/forensicfield/
https://www.linkedin.com/in/forensicfield/
https://forensicfield.tumblr.com/

Forensic Medicine

1. **Forensic Medicine is also known as:**

a.) Medical Jurisprudence

b.) law of medicine

c.) Forensic biology

d.) Medicine

2. **Who is the Father of Legal Medicine?**

a.) Hippocrates

b.) Manu

c.) Paolo Zacchia

d.) Francois-Emmanuelle Fodere

3. **Who is the Father of Surgery?**

a.) Al-Zahrawi

b.) Sushruta

c.) Manu

d.) Hippocrates

4. **'Hidden causes of Disease', A Book on Forensic Pathology is written by:**

a.) Michelangelo

b.) Antonio Benivieni

c.) Andrea Vesalius

d.) Theophile Bonet

5. **Forensic Pathology deals with:**

a.) Interpretation of autopsy findings in a medico legal investigations

b.) It deals with Viscera analysis

c.) It deals with body fluids examination

d.) It deals with medicine

6. **Who is the father of occupational medicine?**

a.) Paracelsus

b.) Mathieu Orfila

c.) Bernardino Ramazzini

d.) Oswald Schmiedeberg

7. **Forensic Medicine deals with the :**

a.) All types of Medicine.

b.) Application of medical knowledge for Legal Proceedings.

c.) Postmortem Reports

d.) For purpose of research

8. **Forensic medicine is a:**

a.) Branch of forensic science

b.) Application of forensic science

c.) A tool

d.) Medium of crime scene investigation

9. An examination of a dead body, by a doctor is called:

a.) Postmortem examination

b.) Autopsy examination

c.) Antemortem examination

d.) Inquest

e.) a & b

10. Forensic Medicine was first practiced in ancient India by:

a.) Aristotle

b.) Manu

c.) Chankya

d.) Charak

11. Study of Death is known as:

a.) Entomology

b.) Forensic Medicine

c.) Toxicology

d.) Thantology

12. First Medicolegal Autopsy was done by:

a.) Bartolomeo da Varignana

b.) Dr. Buckeley

c.) Alfred Swaine Taylor

d.) Johann Ludwig Casper

13. A painter who did some autopsy to learn anatomy of human is:

a.) Pablo Picasso

b.) Vincent van Gogh

c.) Leonardo da Vinci

d.) Claude Monet

14. The word Autopsy is derived from the Greek word "Autopsia". Which means:

a.) Postmortem

b.) Dissection Of Body

c.) The act of seeing for oneself

d.) Operation

15. The application of entomology was first reported by:

a.) Louis Francois Etienne Bergeret

b.) William Spence

c.) William Kirby

d.) Charles Darwin

16. In most cases, forensic entomology will only determine a:

a.) Approximate PMI

b.) Maximum PMI

c.) Minimum PMI

d.) Probable PMI

17. Before 72 hours, Besides of following evidence, livor mortis, algor mortis and rigor mortis are used:

a.) Anthropological

b.) Pathological

c.) Odontological

d.) Entomological

18. Which type of autopsy is performed to solve mysterious and unnatural death?

a.) Clinical Autopsy

b.) Medico legal Autopsy

c.) Anatomical Autopsy

d.) Postmortem

19. Autopsy is done of:

a.) Asked body parts

b.) Contested body parts

c.) Permitted body parts

d.) Whole Body

20. Autopsy is requested by the Police under section:

a.) 174 of Indian evidence act

b.) 174 of criminal procedure code

c.) 174 of Indian Penal Code

d.) 174 of Police Code

21. **Autopsy is requested by the Magistrate under section:**

a.) 176 of Indian evidence act

b.) 176 of criminal procedure code

c.) 176 of Indian Penal Code

d.) 176 of Police Code

22. **The goal of forensic autopsies is:**

a.) For ritual

b.) For identification

c.) For legal purpose

d.) To determine whether death is natural or not

23. **Virtual Autopsy is known as:**

a.) Vitopsy

b.) Video autopsy

c.) Virtopsy

d.) Viropsy

24. **Following tools are used in Virtopsy, except:**

a.) 3D Surface Scanner

b.) MRI

c.) Gas Chromatography

d.) CT Scans

25. **To conduct postmortem examination an authorization letter is necessary in India, from:**

a.) Magistrate

b.) Police Officer

c.) Chief Justice

d.) Any of the above

26. **Best Method of Identification is:**

a.) DNA Fingerprint

b.) Fingerprint

c.) Face Recognition

d.) Old Wounds

27. **The fingerprint pattern may be impaired permanently in case of:**

a.) Eczema

b.) Scalds

c.) Scabies

d.) Leprosy

28. **Which disorder causes no fingerprints since birth?**

a.) Adermatoglyphia

b.) Psoriasis

c.) Eczema

d.) Scleroderma

29. Postmortem examination should be Performed in:

a.) UV Light

b.) IR Light

c.) Day Light

d.) Any of the above

30. Postmortem examination should not be Performed in artificial light if possible, because it might conceal:

a.) Certain shades of color

b.) Truth

c.) Hidden information

d.) Any of the above

31. Time between death and examination of body:

a.) Postmortem Interval

b.) Time since death

c.) Autopsy

d.) Antimortem Interval

32. Procedure of lawful disinterment or digging out of a buried body from the grave is known as:

a.) Cremation

b.) Exhumation

c.) Postmortem

d.) Autopsy

33. Which one of the following is not empowered to order for exhumation:

a.) Subdivisional Magistrate

b.) Tehsildar

c.) District Magistrate

d.) Police Officer

34. What is a time limit for exhumation in India?

a.) 10 years

b.) 20 years

c.) 5 years

d.) No limit

35. Which of the following is not a constituent of embalming fluid?

a.) Eosin

b.) Glycerin

c.) Wax

d.) Formalin

36. After completion of Embalming procedure following can't be made out:

a.) Analysis of Blood

b.) Interpretation of injury/disease

c.) a & b

d.) None of the above is true

37. In Embalming Composition Eosin use as a:

a.) Perfume

b.) Vehicle

c.) Dye

d.) Anticoagulant

38. In Embalming Composition which one of the following is use as a Vehicle:

a.) Water

b.) Glycerin

c.) Formalin

d.) Sodium Borate

39. Minimum quantity of blood required to be preserved for chemical examination is:

a.) 10 ml

b.) 5 ml

c.) 1 ml

d.) 50 ml

40. At what temperature blood should be preserved?

a.) 2^0c

b.) 4^0c

c.) 0⁰c

d.) 1⁰c

41. After death following decreases in blood level:

a.) Potassium

b.) Magnesium

c.) Sodium

d.) Glucose

42. What is the number of true ribs in human body?

a.) 12

b.) 14

c.) 15

d.) 16

43. From vitreous humor, estimation of time since death is done by:

a.) Potassium

b.) Magnesium

c.) Sodium

d.) Glucose

44. If Fluid begins leaked from openings as cell membrane rupture, skin slays off, Time Since Death is:

a.) 1-2 days

b.) 2-4 days

c.) 6-10 days

d.) 30 minutes – 1 hour

45. Potassium deficiency is known as:

a.) Hyperglycemia

b.) Hypocalcaemia

c.) Uremia

d.) Hypokalemia

46. What is professional death sentence:

a.) Erasure of name from the professional register due to any offence

b.) Death sentence passed by court

c.) Death by professional killer

d.) Death in profession

47. Immediate sign of death is:

a.) Fall in body temperature

b.) Cessation of circulation and respiration

c.) Stop breathing

d.) Dilation of pupil

48. In new born babies, during autopsy body cavity to be opened first:

a.) Depend on case

b.) Skull

c.) Abdominal cavity

d.) Bone marrow

49. Greenish discoloration in post mortem is due to:

a.) Methemoglobin

b.) Sulf-Methemoglobin

c.) Aniline

d.) Nitrites

50. Ventricular fibrillation is the most frequent cause of _____.

a.) Sudden Cardiac Arrest

b.) Paralysis

c.) Brain Hemorrhage

d.) Diarrhea

51. Which of the following test compares weight of the lungs to the body:

a.) Hydrostatic Test

b.) Stomach Bowel Test

c.) Breslau's Second Life Test

d.) Fodere's Test

52. This test is done to confirm whether the lungs have undergone respiration in newborn or not:

a.) Hydrostatic Test

b.) Stomach Bowel Test

c.) Breslau's Second Life Test

d.) Fodere's Test

53. Confirmatory sign of Live Birth is:

a.) Closure of Foetal channels

b.) Macerated Skin

c.) Exfoliation of Skin

d.) a & c

54. Skeleton is divided into:

a.) 2

b.) 4

c.) 1

d.) 3

55. "Teeth are Bone", this statement is:

a.) Right

b.) Wrong

c.) Neither right nor wrong

56. 80% bone of Human Skeleton makes of:

a.) Compact Bone

b.) Spongy Bone

c.) Bone Marrow

d.) All of the above

57. If a person is dead within 30 minute from start of fire, reason of death can be:

a.) Asphyxia

b.) Broncho-pneumonia

c.) Burn

d.) Neurogenic shock

58. In a charred body, which of the following is useful in its identification:

a) Comparison of Postmortem X-Rays with dental records

b) Skull Identification

c) Bone marrow

d) Skeletal Features

59. Dental formula for permanent teeth is:

a.) 2102

b.) 2321

c.) 2123

d.) 2121

60. Hardest substance in human body is:

a.) Keratin

b.) Chondrin

c.) Osteon

d.) Enamel

61. Skeletonization will never occur in:

a.) Climate Temperature

b.) Subzero Temperature

c.) Tropical Temperature

d.) Thermodynamic Temperature

62. PM identification is difficult in case of:

a.) Severe burns

b.) Multiple stab wounds

c.) Complete charring

d.) Complete Putrefaction

63. Dry burn is caused by:

a.) Hot liquid or steam

b.) Flame or hot metals

c.) Deep X-Ray or UV-Rays

d.) Strong acids or alkalies

64. Colliquative Liquefaction is seen within:

a.) 1 minute

b.) 1 hour

c.) 1 week

d.) 1 month

65. **Expert witness defines in:**

a.) Sec 45 IEA, 1872

b.) Sec 48 IEA, 1872

c.) Sec 47 IEA, 1872

d.) Sec 46 IEA, 1872

66. **Following Section is related to Dowry Death:**

a.) 300 IPC

b.) 302 IPC

c.) 299 IPC

d.) 304 B IPC

67. **Person is legally dead if he is not found for:**

a.) 30 years

b.) 15 years

c.) 5 years

d.) 7 years

68. **McNaughton's rule given in following section of Indian Penal Code, 1860:**

a.) 84

b.) 85

c.) 86

d.) 87

Forensic Medicine

69. Medical Certificate is a:

a.) Legal Document

b.) Documentary Evidence

c.) Oral evidence

d.) Doctor's Certificate

70. All are exempted from oral testimony, except;

a.) Dying Declaration

b.) Medical evidences of injury as witness

c.) Chemical examination report

d.) Evidence of medical expert in lower court

71. Corpus Delicti Means:

a.) The body of Offence

b.) Dead Corpse

c.) Delicate Corpse

d.) All of the Above

72. Heaviest and largest internal organ of human body is:

a.) Brain

b.) Liver

c.) Kidney

d.) Large intestine

73. Largest organ of the human body is:

a.) Skin

b.) Liver

c.) Large intestine

d.) Kidney

74. Identical Twins may not have:

a.) Identical DNA fingerprint

b.) Identical Blood group

c.) Identical Fingerprint

d.) Identical Appearance

75. Mummification occurs when the climate is:

a.) Hot & Dry

b.) Cold & Dry

c.) Moist

d.) Hot

76. Odour of mummified body is:

a.) Pungent

b.) Putrid

c.) Offensive

d.) Odorless

77. Cerebrospinal Fluid (CSF) in autopsy may be removed by:

a.) Lumbar puncture

b.) Withdrawing Fluid from Cisterna Magna

c.) Puncturing the lateral ventricles directly

d.) All of the above are correct.

78. Radiological signs of fetal death includes all of the following, except:

a.) Overlapping of skull bones

b.) Gross distortion of fetal anatomy

c.) Fever & Cold

d.) Thrombus in fetal heart

79. Specific Gravity of Human body is:

a.) 1.05

b.) 2.08

c.) 1.08

d.) 1.0

80. Closure of coronal suture starts at the age of:

a.) 10-12 years

b.) 15-25 years

c.) 24-40 years

d.) 40-50 years

81. All of the following are found in brain dead patients, except;

a.) Decreased Deep Tendon Reflex

b.) Absent Papillary Reflexes

c.) Complete Apnea

d.) Heart unresponsive to Atropine

82. Following is not a reliable option for estimation of age:

a.) Sternum

b.) Sutural Closure

c.) Frontanelle

d.) Skull Suture

83. Following elements are found in DNA, Except:

a.) Oxygen

b.) Carbon

c.) Sulphur

d.) Phosphorus

84. Statement 1: Teeth are considered best for DNA analysis in Case of Mass disasters.

Statement 2: The cellular material of pulp cavity may remain unaffected.

a.) Both statement is Right

b.) Both statement is Wrong

c.) First part is right second part is wrong

d.) First part is wrong second part is right

85. Union of epiphysis in Head of Humerus occurs at the age of:

a.) 10 years

b.) 17 years

c.) 5 years

d.) 25 years

86. Which one of the following elements is required by our body for normal functioning of some enzymes?

a.) Mercury (Hg)

b.) Zinc (Zn)

c.) Lead (Pb)

d.) Antimony (Sb)

87. Following enzyme is present in tears:

a.) Trypsin

b.) Lysozyme

c.) Maltase

d.) Lipases

88. pH of seminal fluid is

a.) 7.4

b.) 7.0

c.) 2.0

d.) 6.5

89. **Weight of dry Skeleton in adult human males is:**

a.) 10-12kg

b.) 12.5kg-15kg

c.) 2.5kg-5kg

d.) 1kg-3kg

90. **Which of the following is a future of apoptosis?**

a.) Cellular Swelling

b.) Karyolysis

c.) Chromatin Condensation

d.) Associated inflammatory changes

91. **"Nutmeg Liver" refers to**

a.) Chronic Venous congestion

b.) Jaundice

c.) Septicemia

d.) Pneumonia

92. **Fatty change:**

a.) Does not impair cellular function

b.) Is most commonly due to diabetes

c.) Only occurs in lever

d.) Is caused by alcohol by an increase in intracellular alpha glycerol phosphate.

93. The animal eaten parts of the body may be mistaken for ante mortem injury, Which is known as:

a.) Injury

b.) Animal Bite

c.) Pseudo abrasion

d.) Animal abrasion

94. About abrasions following statements are correct, except;

a.) Abrasion on victim may show the length of the fingernails of assailant.

b.) Abrasions are sign of struggle

c.) Abrasions only made by weapon

d.) Gunshot wound also made abrasion

95. Blood usually remains fluid after death, except:

a.) Chronic Venous congestion

b.) Jaundice

c.) Septicemia

d.) Pneumonia

96. Last structure to be autopsied in asphyxial death:

a.) Head

b.) Throax

c.) Abdomen

d.) Neck

97. The Last Sense a dying person loses is:

a.) Sight

b.) Smell

c.) Hearing

d.) Touch

98. The Second Last Sensation a dying person is loses is:

a.) Sight

b.) Smell

c.) Hearing

d.) Touch

99. Chicken Fat Clot is:

a.) Blood clot in chicken

b.) Fatty Acid

c.) Postmortem Blood Clot

d.) Chicken Meat

100. Bertillon system is employed basing on:

a.) Measurement of Hand

b.) Measurement of Leg

c.) Measurement of Body Parts

d.) Measurement of Face

101. **Absorption Elution Technique is used for:**

a.) Detection of seminal stain

b.) Detection of Blood Stain

c.) Detection of vaginal stain

d.) Detection of Faecal stain

102. **The best bones for determining sex are:**

a.) Sternum & Humerus

b.) Clavicle & Tibia

c.) Femur & Ulna

d.) Skull & pelvis

103. **Most useful body part for sex determination is:**

a.) Femur

b.) Pelvis

c.) Tibia fibula

d.) Skull

104. **Sex chromatin is found in:**

a.) Lymphocytes

b.) Erythrocytes

c.) Monocytes

d.) Leucocytes

105. **A body which feels warm & stiff has been dead:**

a.) 2-3 hours

b.) 3-8 hours

c.) After 1 hour

d.) More than 24 hours

106. In Algor Mortis, Algor means:

a.) Death

b.) Dead Body

c.) Coldness

d.) Heat of Body

107. Algor Mortis appears in dead body:

a.) When temperature of the body start to decrease

b.) When temperature of the body start to increase

c.) When temperature of the body constant

d.) When temperature of body is 0^0

108. Rigor Mortis appears First in:

a.) Abdominal wall

b.) Hands

c.) Eyelids

d.) Legs

109. Rigor Mortis can be delayed by:

a.) Obesity

b.) Thinness

c.) Race

d.) Stature

110. Putrefaction is of:

a.) 1 types

b.) 2 types

c.) 3 types

d.) 4 types

111. Black Putrefaction occurs in dead body after:

a.) 4-10 days

b.) 10-20 days

c.) 20-30 days

d.) 30-40 days

112. In Rigor Mortis, Rigor means:

a.) Death

b.) Dead body

c.) Coldness

d.) Rigidity

113. Rigor Mortis Completes in:

a.) 2 hours

b.) 6 hours

c.) 8 hours

d.) 12 hours

114. Immediate rigidity in a group of muscles without passing into stage of primary relaxation is:

a.) Cadaveric Rigidity

b.) Cadaveric Spasm

c.) Rigor Mortis

d.) Mummification

115. Cadaveric Spasm:

a.) Develop immediately after death

b.) Involves individual group of muscles

c.) May develop hours after death

d.) a & b

116. Which one of the following chemical found in the muscles is used and not reproduce after death, is reason of rigor mortis:

a.) Calcium

b.) Glycogen

c.) Potassium

d.) Magnesium

117. Rigor Mortis Appears in dead body:

a.) Within 1-2 hours

b.) Within 2-6 hours

c.) Within 15-30 Minutes

d.) Anytime

118. Arrange in the proper order Rigor Mortis Spreads in the dead body in the following order:

i. Lower Limbs

ii. Chest

iii. Eyelids

iv. Lower Jaw

Code:

a.) (i), (ii), (iii) & (iv)

b.) (iii), (iv), (ii) & (i)

c.) (iv), (ii), (iii) & (i)

d.) (ii), (i), (iv) & (iii)

119. Rigor Mortis is not seen in:

a.) Old Person (above 70 years)

b.) Child

c.) Pregnant women

d.) Fetus (less than 7 months)

120. A dead born fetus (less than 7 month) does not have:

a.) Rigor Mortis

b.) Mummification

c.) Maceration

d.) Adipocere Formation

121. Adipocere may be seen in:

a.) Body exposed to open

b.) Body buried in damp, clay soil

c.) Burial in dry hot air

d.) Prolonged immersion water

122. It develops 15 minutes after death and is the Ist Postmortem sign of death in Caucasian Person:

a.) Livor Mortis

b.) Algor Mortis

c.) Pallor Mortis

d.) Rigor Mortis

123. How many days does it take the eyeball to turn to liquid?

a.) 2 days

b.) 3 days

c.) 6-10 days

d.) 1 week

124. Pallor Mortis occurs in:

a.) Person with dark skin

b.) Person with Tan Skin

c.) Person with Normal Skin

d.) Person With Light/White Skin

125. In "Pallor Mortis", "Pallor" Means:

a.) Rigidness

b.) Paleness

c.) Stoppage of Pulse

d.) Brown Bluish Discolouration

126. Livor Mortis appears in dead body:

a.) Within 20-30 minutes

b.) Within 1-2 hours

c.) Within 2-6 hours

d.) Anytime

127. Reddish-bluish staining of low lying dependent regions of the body, known as:

a.) Rigor Mortis

b.) Livor Mortis

c.) Algor Mortis

d.) Pallor Mortis

128. How long after death does lividity become permanent?

a.) 30 minutes

b.) 1 hours

c.) 2 hours

d.) 8 hours

129. Luminol reacts with hydrogen salt and forms in _____ Luminol Test:

a.) Anion

b.) Cation

c.) Di-anion

d.) Ion

130. The cooling of body is best represented by following curve when temperature and time does not match:

a.) Sigmoid Curve

b.) Circular

c.) Linear

d.) Any of the Above

131. The temperature of the dead body is measured using:

a.) Medical Thermometer

b.) Thanatometer

c.) Pacifier Thermometer

d.) Infrared Thermometer

132. The Temperature ideally preferred to preserve the body for autopsy is:

a.) 4⁰c

b.) 0⁰c

c.) -4⁰c

d.) 1⁰c

133. Chronological order of Postmortem changes after death is:

a.) Loss of reflexes, foul smell, adipocere and hypostasis

b.) Loss of reflexes, hypostasis, foul smell, and adipocere

c.) Foul smell, hypostasis, Loss of reflexes and adipocere

d.) Adipocere, Loss of reflexes, foul smell and hypostasis

134. Hypostasis is last for _____ :

a.) Few Hours

b.) Days

c.) Week

d.) Months

135. _____ is used as medicine in Mental illnesses like Schizophrenia, Bipolar disorder and Depression:

a.) Benzene

b.) Lithium

c.) Arsenic

d.) Barium

136. Gene Mutations caused by chemicals initiates the process of carcinogenesis. Which kinds of genes are mutated in this process?

a.) Oncogenes

b.) Protooncogenes

c.) Tumor suppressor genes

d.) b & c

137. Rule of Hasse is used to determine:

a.) Age of fetus

b.) The age of adult

c.) For identification

d.) Height of person

138. Time since death is calculated by multiplying drop in rectal temperature with:

a.) 0.67

b.) 2

c.) 0.37

d.) 0.46

139. Rectal temperature does not fall till what time after death?

a.) 15-30 minutes

b.) 30-60 minutes

c.) 60-90 minutes

d.) Immediately after death

140. The rate of cooling of dead body in normal weather is:

a.) 1.5°F/hour

b.) 4.5°F/hour

c.) 2.5°F/hour

d.) 0.5°F/hour

141. The following situations are associated with rise of temperature after death:

a.) Heat Stroke

b.) Strychnine poisoning

c.) Septicemia

d.) All of the above

142. Most accurate place to take the body temperature of the deceased:

a.) Liver

b.) Kidney

c.) Intestine

d.) Brain

143. Rate of cooling helps in determining:

a.) Place of death

b.) Time of death

c.) Cause of death

d.) Manner of death

144. Time when the cooling of the body is completed may vary according to:

a.) The medium in which it is kept after death

b.) Condition of the body itself

c.) Manner of death

d.) All of the above

145. Following bodies retains heat longer than usual:

a.) Fat Bodies

b.) Die from Lightning

c.) a & b

d.) Time is same for all types of dead bodies

146. Rigor mortis starts when muscle ATP is reduced below:

a.) 15%

b.) 5%

c.) 50%

d.) 100%

147. _____ is the main source of energy for muscle contraction:

a.) ATP (Adenosine Triposhphate)

b.) Food

c.) Water

d.) Vitamin's

148. After death, generation of ATP stops, but consumption of it :

a.) also stops

b.) Continues

c.) Depends on body

d.) Constant

149. Depressed fracture of skull results from blows with:

a.) Heavy object with small striking surface

b.) Heavy object with large striking surface

c.) Small object with heavy striking surface

d.) Large object with light striking surface

150. Greenstick fracture is:

a.) Wrist fracture

b.) Fatigue fracture

c.) Part of cortex is intact and other part is crumpled

d.) Spiral fracture of long bone

151. Boxer's Fracture is:

a.) Fracture of first metacarpal base

b.) Fracture of fifth metacarpal neck

c.) Fracture of third metacarpal neck

d.) Fracture of first metacarpal neck

152. Hyoid fracture is common in:

a.) Choking

b.) Hanging

c.) Strangulation

d.) b & c

153. All are reason for death due to suffocation, except:

a.) Smothering

b.) Throttling

c.) Choking

d.) Gagging

154. Fracture in hyoid bone and larynx indicate:

a.) Suicidal Throttling

b.) Accidental Throttling

c.) Homicidal Throttling

d.) Manual Strangulation

155. Lynching is:

a.) Practiced in North America

b.) Hanging on Tree

c.) Practiced by white people on Negros

d.) All

156. Bleeding from the nostril, Mouth and ears is common in:

a.) Hanging

b.) Strangulation by Ligature

c.) Garroting

d.) Choking

157. In _____, a loop of thin string is thrown around the neck of the victim from back.

a.) Garroting

b.) Burking

c.) Bansdola

d.) Strangulation

158. Spanish windlass is practiced in which form of strangulation:

a.) Bansdola

b.) Garroting

c.) Throttling

d.) Mugging

159. Maximum congestion is seen in:

a.) Hanging

b.) Choking

c.) Strangulation

d.) Drowning

160. _____ is a form of strangulation where the neck is compressed in between two bamboos or other sticks, one in front and one from the back.

a.) Garroting

b.) Burking

c.) Bansdola

d.) Strangulation

161. Bansdola is a form of:

a.) Homicidal Suffocation

b.) Homicidal Strangulation

c.) Homicidal Choking

d.) Homicidal Hanging

162. Appearance of simulating ligature mark on the neck due to the postmortem staining is:

a.) Garroting

b.) Burking

c.) Bansdola

d.) Pseudo Strangulation

163. Holding the neck of victim when bend his elbow is known as:

a.) Mugging

b.) Bansdola

c.) Garrotting

d.) Throttling

164. "Café coronary" is

a.) A type of death due to choking

b.) Death due to drowning

c.) Sudden death

d.) Death due to Poisoning

165. A person suddenly starts coughing and choking while eating his food and died shortly after. Reason of death is:

a.) Choking

b.) Gagging

c.) Smothering

d.) Trauma

166. Impotence quad hoc means?

a.) Medically impotent

b.) Legally impotent

c.) Impotent toward a particular woman

d.) All of the above

167. Best indicator of antimortem drowning is:

a.) Froth In Nostrils

b.) Water in Lungs

c.) Hemolysis

d.) Water in stomach

168. Death occurs faster in:

a.) Salt Water Drowning

b.) Fresh Water Drowning

c.) Sea Water Drowning

d.) Warm Water Drowning

169. Gettler's Test is used to diagnose death due to:

a.) Hanging

b.) Strangulation

c.) Burns

d.) Drowning

170. Which of the following is not true about fresh water drowning?

a.) Hyperkalemia

b.) Hypovolemia

c.) Ventricular fibrillation

d.) Hemolysis

171. Which of the following is not seen in salt water drowning?

a.) Hyperkalemia

b.) Progressive Hypovolemia

c.) Circulatory collapse

d.) Acute Pulmonary Edema

172. Washer man's hand and feet are commonly seen in case of drowning in:

a.) 2 – 3 hrs.

b.) 24 – 48 hrs.

c.) 18 – 24 hrs.

d.) 6 – 12 hrs.

173. Autopsy findings of Drowning in sea water is:

a.) Salty water in stomach

b.) High Potassium in left Heart

c.) High calcium in heart

d.) All of the Above

174. In drowning, the epidermis of the hands and feet is separated in the form of gloves and stocking after:

a.) 2 min

b.) 2 hrs.

c.) 2 weeks

d.) 2 months

175. What is dry drowning?

a.) Death occurs in few days of submersion episode

b.) Death occurs due to sudden immersion in cold water

c.) Water does not enter in lungs because of laryngeal spasm

d.) Seen in alcoholics due to drowning in shallow pool

176. Cutis anserine seen in :

a.) Strangulation

b.) Garroting

c.) Drowning

d.) Throttling

177. Gall bladder will be _____ in starvation in postmortem.

a.) Distended

b.) Normal

c.) Stretched

d.) Thick Walled

178. A young lady was found dead. Her body was cold & complete stiff. The expected time pass since death is:

a.) 2-4 hrs.

b.) 4-6 hrs.

c.) 6-10 hrs.

d.) More than 10 hrs.

179. Viscera should be kept/Preserved in :

a.) Glass bottle

b.) Plastic container

c.) Paper bag

d.) Steel Can

180. Which disorder/disease is rare in women compared to the men:

a.) Osteoporosis

b.) Nyctalopia

c.) Down Syndrome

d.) Color Blindness

181. Permanent Infirmity means:

a.) A dangerous stab wound

b.) Loss of Organ Function

c.) Loss of an Organ

d.) b & c

182. The positive finding of burial of a living person is:

a.) Marked pulmonary oedema

b.) Rigidity of Body

c.) Earth or sand in trachea and bronchi

d.) Congestion of liver and spleen

183. Gordon's Classification deals with-

a.) Stature

b.) Fingerprints

c.) Death

d.) Footprint

184. In wild life Forensics, identification of animals done by

a.) Body Features

b.) Pug Marks

c.) Color

d.) Twigs

185. Illegal way of trafficking animals:

a.) Poaching

b.) Trafficking

c.) Kidnapping

d.) Smuggling

186. Psychological autopsy is?

a.) Autopsy of brain and spinal cord

b.) To inquire about the psychiatric illness of the deceased

c.) Assessment to the mental state of deceased person before death

d.) All of the above

187. Coup-Contrecoup Injury is:

a.) Damage to the brain on both sides

b.) Accidental injury on leg

c.) Dislocation of bones

d.) Paralysis

188. Duret Hemorrhages are found in:

a.) Liver

b.) Brain

c.) Kidney

d.) Heart

189. Brain Bleed is known as:

a.) Intracranial Hemorrhage

b.) Subarachnoid Hemorrhage

c.) Epidural Hematoma

d.) Subdural Hematoma

190. Most common type of Intracranial hemorrhage:

a.) Epidural Hemorrhage

b.) Subarachnoid Hemorrhage

c.) Epidural Hematoma

d.) Subdural Hematoma

191. Statement 1- Hemorrhage: Copious discharge of blood from the blood vessels.

Statement 2- Hematoma: Localized collection of blood in the tissues, usually to clotted or partially clotted.

a.) Statement 1 is right while Statement 2 is wrong

b.) Statement 1 is right while Statement 2 is wrong

c.) Both Statements is Right

d.) Both Statements is Wrong

192. Following tests are associated with cessation of circulation, except:

a.) Magnus Test

b.) I-Card's Test

c.) Takayama Test

d.) Diaphanous Test

193. Magnus test also known as:

a.) Fingernail Test

b.) I-Card's Test

c.) Ligature Test

d.) Transillumination Test

194. Transillumiation Test is also known as:

a.) Fingernail Test

b.) Diaphanous Test

c.) I Card's Test

d.) Ligature Test

195. Which test is associated with cessation of Breathing?

a.) Feather Test

b.) Mirror Test

c.) Winslow's Test

d.) All of the Above

196. Wreden's test is to demonstrate-

a.) Live birth

b.) Insanity

c.) Putrefaction

d.) Assault

197. Breslau's second life test utilizes:

a.) Liver

b.) Stomach

c.) Ear

d.) Lungs

198. For examination of diatoms sample should collect from:

a.) Nasal Cavity

b.) Epithelial Cells

c.) Bone Marrow

d.) Blood

199. Best body part for taking sample for diatom test:

a.) Lungs

b.) Stomach

c.) From any part of body

d.) Bone Marrow in Femur

200. Diatoms are:

a.) Algae

b.) Parasites

c.) Bacteria

d.) Fungi

201. Dirt Collar is seen in:

a.) Drowning

b.) Firearm Entry wound

c.) Mob Lynching

d.) All

202. Wounds on the left hand are suggestive of:

a.) Fabricated wound

b.) Defense wound

c.) Self-inflicted wound

d.) None

203. Postmortem Rigidity first starts in:

a.) Upper Eyelids

b.) Fingers

c.) Hands

d.) Mouth

204. Fracture-a-la-signature (or **signature fracture**) is a _____:

a.) Depressed Skull Fracture

b.) Finger Fracture

c.) Parkinson's

d.) None of the above

205. Gutter fracture can be seen in:

a.) Accident case

b.) Bullet injury

c.) Crushed skull

d.) Sharp weapon injury

206. Pond Fracture is also known as:

a.) Gutter fracture

b.) Hinge fracture

c.) Ping-Pong Ball Fracture

d.) None of the above

207. Pond fracture is seen in:

a.) Neonates and young children

b.) Adults

c.) Both

d.) None of the above

208. Statement 1: Children have 20 teeth, called temporary or milk teeth.

Statement 2: They are strong, broad and heavy.

a.) Both Statements are wrong

b.) Both Statements are Right

c.) Statement 1 is wrong but Statement 2 is right

d.) Statement 1 is Right but Statement 2 is wrong

209. Adipocere is Hydrogenation or saponification of fats, which occurs in:

a.) Bodies immersed in water

b.) Body buried in Soil

c.) Burnt body

d.) Body exposed in air

210. Which is true about Adipocere:

a.) Also called saponification

b.) Sweetish smell

c.) Occurs due to gradual hydrolysis and hydrogenation of fats

d.) All of the above

211. Adipocere formation is an _____ :

a.) Biochemical Change

b.) Bacterial Process

c.) Enzymatic Process

d.) Accidental Phenomenon

212. The following term is used when Fetus die in the womb and its skin becomes soggy, wet, soft to touch:

a.) Adipocere

b.) Putrefaction

c.) Saponification

d.) Maceration

213. Spalding sign seen in:

a.) Poisoning

b.) Drowning

c.) Maceration

d.) Adipocere

214. Putrefaction is:

a.) Autolysis of the body

b.) Cooling of the body

c.) Stiffening of the body

d.) Foul smelling of the body

215. Putrefaction is facilitated by all, Except:

a.) Very high temperature

b.) Fresh air

c.) Moist environment

d.) Grave

216. Which solutions should be inject for the preservation of dead body and delaying the process of putrefaction for some time:

a.) Formaldehyde

b.) Anesthesia

c.) Ceftriaxone Injection

d.) Fluconazole

217. Color changes of Putrefaction are first observed in the:

a.) Right iliac fossa

b.) Popliteal fossa

c.) Cubital fossa

d.) Armpits

218. A process after death in which a corpse preserved through desiccation is known as:

a.) Skeletalisation

b.) Mummification

c.) Putrefaction

d.) Embalming

219. Place of destroyed tattoo mark can be inferred from the presence of pigment in:

a.) Outer layer of skin

b.) Epidermis

c.) Lymph nodes Regional

d.) Endodermis

220. Main cause of death in severe burn cases is:

a.) Fever

b.) Bacterial infection

c.) Dehydration

d.) b & c

221. Which one of the following will be a third degree burn?

a.) Burns extends through all the skin layers and tissue

b.) 90% of the body is burnt

c.) 5% are of body is burnt

d.) Joints of body are burnt

222. Which of the followings affect the seriousness of electric burn?

a.) Type of electric current

b.) Exposed body surface area

c.) Age of the victim

d.) All of the above

223. Which finding in the body is suggestive of antemortem burns?

a.) 100% burns

b.) Soot in airways

c.) Flexion of joints

d.) None of the above

224. Casper's Dictum is used for:

a.) Estimation of Time since death

b.) Cause of death

c.) Identification of body

d.) All of the above

225. Bones begin to decompose after death in :

a.) After 3 years

b.) After 6 Months

c.) After 1 week

d.) After 1 years

226. The speed of decomposition depend upon:

a.) Body

b.) Age

c.) Nature of death

d.) Environment

e.) All Of The Above

227. The mechanism of death from cold is:

a.) Carboxy hemoglobin formation

b.) Respiratory Enzyme inhabitation

c.) CNS failure

d.) Paralysis

228. First internal organ to Putrefy is:

a.) Liver

b.) Kidney

c.) Brain

d.) Larynx/Trachea

229. First sign of putrefaction is found:

a.) Below the liver

b.) Heart

c.) Spleen

d.) Kidney

230. Order of Putrefaction in Human body is:

a.) Heart-Brain-Uterus-Spleen

b.) Spleen-Brain-Heart-Uterus

c.) Heart-Spleen-Brain-Uterus

d.) Uterus-Heart-Spleen-Brain

231. Last Organ to Putrefy

a.) Testes

b.) Uterus/Prostate

c.) Ovary

d.) Kidney

232. Putrefaction occurs over the ceacal area after around:

a.) 12 hours

b.) 12-24 hours

c.) 24-28 hours

d.) 3 days

233. Chadwick's Sign is:

a.) Red bruise on Vagina

b.) Blue Coloration of Vagina

c.) Bruises on Body

d.) Stiffing of Body

234. Which locus is used for determining both male and female gender in DNA fingerprinting?

a.) DYS 19

b.) DYS-STR 393

c.) Y-plex Ladder

d.) Amelogenin

235. Joule Burns are seen in:

a.) Electrocution

b.) Burn by flame

c.) Lightining

d.) 3rd degree burn

236. Suspended animation (when subject is alive but shows no sign of life) may be seen in:

a.) Hanging

b.) Strangulation

c.) Electrocution

d.) Murder

237. Confirmatory Sign of being burned alive is:

a.) Smell of flammable substance from body

b.) Burnt Clothes

c.) Carbon particles in terminal bronchioles

d.) Burnt skin

238. The characteristic difference between antemortem and postmortem clot is:

a.) Color

b.) Elasticity

c.) Texture

d.) Adhesion to vessel wall

239. Difference between antemortem and postmortem wound is:

a.) Presence Of Chloride In Blister

b.) Presence Of Cynhaemoglobin

c.) Extravasation

d.) Stain Removal Mechanically

240. Kevorkian sign is seen in?

a.) Heart

b.) Pupil

c.) Retinal Vessels

d.) Cornea

241. Kevorkian sign is seen by using an?

a.) Microscope

b.) Ophthalmoscope

c.) Magnifying Glass

d.) All

242. Kevorkian sign is a _____.

a.) Postmortem change

b.) Antemortem change

c.) Perimortem change

d.) All of the above

243. Kevorkian sign appears in dead body_____.

a.) It appears within hour after death and lasts for about 24 hour.

b.) It appears within minutes after death and lasts for about 1 hour.

c.) It appears within hour after death and lasts for about 7 hour.

d.) It appears within seconds after death and lasts for about 4 hour.

244. Whiplash injury is caused due to:

a.) Injury on Head

b.) Acute hypertension of Spine

c.) a & c

d.) Hand injury

245. Hegar's sign is for the detection of

a.) Early sign of Pregnancy

b.) Dead Foetus

c.) Complication of Pregnancy

d.) Virginity

246. Failure of function of Brain in case of :

a.) Asphyxia

b.) Coma

c.) Syncope

d.) All of the above

247. Failure of function of Heart in case of :

a.) Asphyxia

b.) Coma

c.) Syncope

d.) All of the above

248. Failure of respiratory System in case of :

a.) Asphyxia

b.) Coma

c.) Syncope

d.) All of the above

249. All may cause traumatic asphyxia, except:

a.) Railway Accident

b.) Accidental Strangulation

c.) Road Accident

d.) All of the above

250. _____ is a general term referring to inadequate supply of Oxygen to the tissues or an impairment of the cellular utilization of oxygen for any reason.

a.) Hypoxemia

b.) Hypoxia

c.) Anoxia

d.) None

251. Marbling is due to:

a.) Clotting of blood in veins

b.) Lightening

c.) Veins becoming visible due to decomposition of blood

d.) All of the above

252. Types of hypoxia include:

a.) Hypoxic hypoxia

b.) Anemic hypoxic

c.) Cytotoxic/Histotoxic hypoxia

d.) Stagnant hypoxia

e.) All Of the Above

253. In general, what type of drugs are psychotropic medications?

a.) Acidic Drugs

b.) Basic Drugs

c.) Neutral Drugs

d.) Methylated Drugs

254. _____refers only to decreased carriage of oxygen in the arterial blood.

a.) Hypoxemia

b.) Hypoxia

c.) Anoxia

d.) None

255. Refractive index of hair is determined by:

a.) Microscopic examination

b.) Florence Test

c.) Beckline Method

d.) All of the above

256. Hair _____ to grow after death.

a.) Start

b.) Cease

c.) Continue

d.) More

257. Features which distinguishes human hair from animal hair is:

a.) Equal diameter of medulla and cortex

b.) Medulla is 1/3 or less of the shaft diameter

c.) Pigments

d.) Medulla is half or more of the shaft diameter

258. Burking is a particular method of homicidal smothering and traumatic asphyxiation, which is named after:

a.) Burke and Hare

b.) Burk and king

c.) Burke and hang

d.) Burke and Burke

259. Burking is derived from:

a.) Place

b.) Style use for murder

c.) Weapon used for murder

d.) Person

260. The postmortem finding seen in smothering:

a.) Fracture of the body of hyoid

b.) Abrasion on the inner side of the mouth

c.) Thyroid fracture

d.) Curved mark on the neck

261. Sexual asphyxia is associated with:

a.) Sadism

b.) Fetishism

c.) Masochism

d.) Voyeurism

262. Sexual asphyxia is:

a.) Suicidal Death

b.) Homicidal death

c.) Natural death

d.) Accidental death

263. The bleeding and tears from genitalia is indicative of:

a.) Abortion

b.) Instrumentation

c.) Forced Sexual Intercourse

d.) Self-inflicted injury

264. Bar Bodies are not seen in:

a.) Down's Syndrome

b.) Klinefelter Syndrome

c.) Marfan's Syndrome

d.) Turner Syndrome

265. Turner syndrome occurs in:

a.) Male

b.) Female

c.) Both of the above

d.) None of the above

266. Tribadism is :

a.) Female Homosexuality

b.) Male Homosexuality

c.) Homosexuality

d.) None of the Above

267. Two Bar Bodies are seen in

a.) XXX

b.) XX

c.) XO

d.) XXY

268. Cephalic Index is useful for the determination of

a.) Age

b.) Race

c.) Sex

d.) Face

269. Race can be determined by the:

a.) Complexion

b.) Voice

c.) Fingerprint

d.) Footprint

270. Classical disorder of sex chromosome is:

a.) Down's Syndrome

b.) Klinefelter Syndrome

c.) Marfan's Syndrome

d.) All of the above

271. Klinefelter Syndrome occurs in:

a.) Male

b.) Female

c.) Both of the above

d.) None of the above

272. Earliest bone to ossify is:

a.) Femur

b.) Clavicle

c.) Tibia fibula

d.) Pelvis

273. For bone age calculation in individuals aged 18-22 years, Radiographs are done of :

a.) Clavicle

b.) Elbow

c.) Wrist

d.) Knee

274. Pearson's Formula is Used for:

a.) Age

b.) Race

c.) Sex

d.) Stature

275. Which of the organ is commonly affected by shock waves?

a.) Heart

b.) Lungs

c.) Liver

d.) Brain

276. Which is not a Thermal Injury?

a.) Heat stroke

b.) Scalds

c.) Contusion

d.) Hypothermia

277. Which is not a Mechanical Injury?

a.) Abrasion

b.) Incised Wound

c.) Firearm Wound

d.) Burns

278. Lichtenberg Figures is an external lesion seen in?

a.) Heat stroke

b.) Radiation Injury

c.) Lightning

d.) Electrocution

279. Following markings are seen in Lichtenberg figures?

a.) Burning marking

b.) Blisters on skin

c.) Burned and patchy skin

d.) Superficial, thin, tortuous markings

280. Which type of pattern seen in Lichtenberg figures?

a.) Circles

b.) Sketchy lines

c.) Thorn like pattern

d.) Fern Leaf

281. Lichtenberg figures are also known as?

a.) Lightning figures

b.) Filigree burns

c.) Radiography Burns

d.) All of the above

282. Hanging is:

a.) Suspension of body by ligature after death

b.) Obliteration of air passage by external factor

c.) Mechanical interference to respiration

d.) Suspension of body by a ligature around the neck, body weight acting as constricting force

283. Ligature mark in hanging is:

a.) Oval

b.) Circular

c.) Oblique

d.) Straight

284. "Le Facie Sympathique" is seen in:

a.) Hanging

b.) Homicide

c.) Dowry Death

d.) Poisoning Case

285. A horizontal ligature mark is seen in the neck in case of hanging:

a.) In partial Hanging

b.) Throttling

c.) When a fixed loop with a single knot at the back of the head

d.) When a fixed loop with a single knot at the chin

286. In Judicial Hanging, fracture of vertebral column is usually seen between:

a.) C1 And C2

b.) C2 And C3

c.) C4 And C5

d.) C5 And C6

287. Simon sign is mainly seen in:

a.) Forcible Rape

b.) Oral Intercourse

c.) Infanticide

d.) Complete hanging

288. Coma occurs rapidly in hanging if ligature completely obstructs:

a.) Vertebral Arteries

b.) Jugular Veins

c.) Carotid Arteries

d.) None of the Above

289. When the body is suspended from a high point of suspension and feet are not touching ground, it is called:

a.) Complete Hanging

b.) Partial Hanging

c.) Typical Hanging

d.) Atypical Hanging

290. A male suspended himself. A ligature found around his neck and the knot was situated in region of occipital area this is known as:

a.) Typical Hanging

b.) Atypical Hanging

c.) Strangulation

d.) Asphyxia

291. In typical hanging knot is present at:

a.) In front of ear

b.) Mastoid area

c.) Occipital Area

d.) Thyroid cartilage

292. In case of typical hanging, post mortem hypostasis is seen in:

a.) Hands and forearms

b.) Legs and feet

c.) Private parts

d.) a & b

293. When the knot of the ligature is elsewhere, such as; right or left side of neck, it is known as:

a.) Typical Hanging

b.) Atypical Hanging

c.) Complete Hanging

d.) Partial Hanging

294. When some part of the body touches the ground, like; knees, feet, etc. It is known as:

a.) Complete Hanging

b.) Partial Hanging

c.) Typical Hanging

d.) Atypical Hanging

295. Tardieu spots in hanging are not seen in:

a.) Scalp

b.) Eyebrow

c.) Chest wall

d.) Face

296. Tardieu spot disappear after:

a.) 1 hour

b.) 2 hour

c.) As rigor set in

d.) never

297. Increased salivation is seen in death due to:

a.) Strangulation

b.) Hanging

c.) Drowning

d.) Choking

298. A confirm sign of antemortem hanging is:

a.) Swollen and protrude tongue

b.) Protrude tongue and congested eyes

c.) A thin line of congestion of eyes hemorrhage along the edges of ligature mark

d.) Swollen hand and foot

299. In Undertaker's Fracture, Tearing of vertebral column is usually seen between:

a.) C1 And C2

b.) C2 And C3

c.) C4 And C5

d.) C6 And C7

300. Undertaker's Fracture is basically a:

a.) Antemortem Fracture

b.) Postmortem Fracture

c.) Perimortem Fracture

d.) Fracture

301. Postmortem fracture differs from antemortem fracture by all, Except:

a.) Absence Of Bleeding

b.) Absence Of Granulation At Fracture Site

c.) Laceration Over Skin

d.) Absence Of Callus

302. Hangman's Fracture is mainly caused due to impacts of high force causing extension of the neck and great axial load onto the:

a.) C1 And C2

b.) C2

c.) C3

d.) C6 And C7

303. Teardrop sign is seen in:

a.) Fracture media wall of orbit

b.) Fracture lateral wall of orbit

c.) Fracture floor of orbit

d.) Fracture roof of orbit

304. Fracture in root of orbit is caused by:

a.) Blow on forehead

b.) Blow on Lower Jaw

c.) Fall on backside

d.) Blow on parietal region

305. Concussion causes:

a.) Small hemorrhages and swelling of brain tissues

b.) Momentary interruption of brain function with/without loss of consciousness

c.) Tearing or shearing of brain structures

d.) Bruising of the brain

306. Which one of the following is not a skull fracture type:

a.) Linear

b.) Depressed

c.) Basal

d.) Diffused axonal

307. Le Forte's Fracture would include all of the following, except:

a.) Maxilla

b.) Mandible

c.) Zygoma

d.) Nasal bones

308. Bumper fracture is:

a.) Primary Impact injury

b.) Secondary impact injury

c.) Tertiary impact injury

d.) Secondary injury

309. Motor Cyclist fracture also known as hinge fracture, occurs when:

a.) Comminuted fracture of the vault

b.) Skull base divided into 2 halves

c.) Ring fracture

d.) Gutter fracture

310. Sparrow foot marks are associated with which type of injury:

a.) Motor cyclist fracture

b.) Steering wheel impact

c.) Wind screen impact

d.) Under-running fracture

311. In Lacerated wound the hair bulb is:

a.) Cut

b.) Crushed

c.) Dragged

d.) Lacerated

312. Lanugo hair grows on:

a.) Body of human fetus in womb

b.) Body of an adult

c.) Body of an animal

d.) All of the above

313. Lanugo Hairs are:

a.) Pigmented

b.) Medullae

c.) Complex Scale Patterns

d.) Thin and Soft

314. In 'Crippen case', body of Cora Crippen was identified by:

a.) Tattoo mark

b.) Scar Tissue

c.) Color of eyes

d.) DNA Test

315. Which of the following is true regarding Superfecundation?

a.) The second fetus born later.

b.) Fertilization of ovum in an already pregnant woman

c.) Both ova do not always develop to maturity

d.) All of the above

316. Rigor mortis does not occur in fetus less than:

a.) 9 month

b.) 12 month

c.) 8 month

d.) 7 month

317. Putrefaction is brought about in a dead body by:

a.) Viruses

b.) Bacterial Action

c.) Moths

d.) Temperature

318. Chief agent for bacterial putrefaction is:

a.) E. coli

b.) B. fragilis

c.) C. Welchii

d.) Staph Aureus

319. Following organisms are responsible for putrefaction:

a.) Staphylococcus

b.) Streptococcus

c.) C. Welchii

d.) All of the Above

320. Putrefaction is slower in:

a.) Water

b.) Ground

c.) Moist Place

d.) None

321. Putrefaction is replaced Occasionally by:

a.) Mummification

b.) Rigor Mortis

c.) Adipocere Formation

d.) a & c

322. Putrefactive gases are all except:

a.) CO_2

b.) NO_2

c.) H_2S

d.) NH_3

323. The dead body start emitting unpleasant and foul smell due to formation and collection of following decomposition gas:

a.) H_2S

b.) Methane

c.) CO_2

d.) NH_3

e.) All of the Above

324. Decomposition in human body starts in:

a.) Fresh Stage

b.) Post-Decay Stage

c.) Decay Stage

d.) Bloat Stage

325. Postmortem hemolysis due to bacterial enzyme:

a.) Lecithinase

b.) Phospholipase

c.) Streptokinase

d.) Hyaluronidase

326. Tsunami Lung is :

a.) Death by explosion of lung, as if a tsunami is caused within the body

b.) Severe systemic infections following aspiration pneumonia caused by near drowning in a Tsunami

c.) Death due to drowning in Tsunami

d.) Finding of both lungs separated completely from their bronchial attachments, seen most often in tsunamis.

327. _____ is fertilization of 2 ova discharged from the ovary at the same period by 2 separate acts of coitus committed at short intervals.

a.) Superfertilization

b.) Superfecundation

c.) Superfetation

d.) Surrogacy

328. Contusion becomes yellow due to:

a.) Bilirubin in the 5th day

b.) Reduced hemoglobin in the 3rd day

c.) Biliverdin in the 5th day

d.) Bilirubin in the 1st day

329. _____ is the most reliable method for estimating blood alcohol level.

a.) Cavett's Test

b.) Breath Alcohol Anaylzer

c.) Kozelka and Hine Test

d.) Gas Liquid Chromatography

330. Tachie noire refers to:

a.) Postmortem staining

b.) Flaccidity of eyeball

c.) Wrinkled dusty sclera

d.) Maggot growth

331. Retraction balls after trauma are seen in:

a.) Brain

b.) Lung

c.) Spleen

d.) Liver

332. Apolexy is:

a.) Learning disability

b.) Insanity leading to commitment of a crime

c.) Sudden onset of bleeding in the brain

d.) Injury to the brain due to trauma

333. Brain hemorrhage limited by sutures:

a.) EDH (Epidural Hematoma)

b.) SAH (Subarachnoid hemorrhage)

c.) SDH (Subdural Hematoma)

d.) ICH (Intracerebral Hemorrhage)

334. Petechial Hemorrhages may be seen in case of:

a.) Peritoneum

b.) Pericardium

c.) Meninges

d.) All of the above

335. Traumatic Bleeding may include all, except:

a.) EDH (Epidural Hematoma)

b.) SAH (Subarachnoid hemorrhage)

c.) SDH (Subdural Hematoma)

d.) ICH (Intracerebral Hemorrhage)

336. Vibices is also known as:

a.) Poisoning

b.) Postmortem Staining

c.) Bruises

d.) Tumor

337. Mineralization of teeth begins at:

a.) Crown and progresses towards root

b.) Root and progresses towards crown

c.) Simultaneously at root and crown

d.) Begins in the center

338. Rave drug is _____?

a.) Poppy seeds

b.) Ecstasy

c.) Cannabis Sativa

d.) Heroin

339. Which of the following is used for Narcoanalysis?

a.) Scopolamine (Hyoscine)

b.) Sodium thiopental (Sodium Pentothal)

c.) Amobarbital (Amytal Sodium)

d.) Secobarbital sodium (Seconal)

e.) All of the above

340. Fertilization of a second ovum in a woman who is already pregnant is:

a.) Superfertilization

b.) Superfecundation

c.) Superfetation

d.) Surrogacy

341. Drug that is absolutely contradicted in pregnancy are:

a.) Diazepam

b.) Aspirin

c.) Acetaminophen

d.) Penicillin

342. Molecular Death refers to...

a.) Death of Cells.

b.) Complete and irreversible cessation of the function of the brain, heart and the lungs.

c.) Death of molecules.

d.) Body stops working.

343. Somatic Death refers to:

a.) Death of Cells.

b.) Complete and irreversible cessation of the function of the brain, heart and the lungs.

c.) Death of molecules.

d.) Body stops working.

344. Apparent Death refers to:

a.) Death of Cells.

b.) Complete and irreversible cessation of the function of the brain, heart and the lungs.

c.) Death of molecules.

d.) That state in which breathing and functions of the heart are slowed down.

345. Somatic Death Also known as:

a.) Molecular death

b.) Clinical Death

c.) Cellular Death

d.) Sudden Death

346. Molecular Death Also known as:

a.) Molecular death

b.) Clinical Death

c.) Cellular Death

d.) Sudden Death

347. Self-inflicted injury are known as:

a.) Fabricated Injury

b.) Forged Injury

c.) Fictious Injury

d.) All of the above

348. Blunt injury to abdomen:

a.) Rarely Need Urgent Laparotomy

b.) May Cause Intestinal Obstruction

c.) May Cause Peritonitis

d.) May Cause Gastroduodenal Ulceration

349. Death in blunt trauma chest is due to:

a.) Tracheobronchial Injury

b.) Pulmonary Contusions

c.) Rupture Esophagus

d.) Chylothorax

350. Which hormone is not released in Trauma:

a.) Glucagon

b.) GH

c.) Thyroxin

d.) ADH

351. Postmortem Luminescence is caused by:

a.) Oleander

b.) Armillaria

c.) Mercury

d.) Bacteria

352. Postmortem Luminescence is usually due to contamination of following bacteria:

a.) Cl. Welchii

b.) E. Coli

c.) Photobacterium Fischeri

d.) All of the above

353. Following Disease is caused by bacteria in Human Eye:

a.) Glaucoma

b.) Xerophthalmia

c.) Trachoma

d.) Protanopia

354. Hensen's cells are found in:

a.) Liver

b.) Spleen

c.) Ear

d.) Eye

355. Which one is not a clinical feature of raised intracranial features of raised intracranial tension?

a.) Headache

b.) Insomnia

c.) Bradycardia

d.) Papilloedema

356. Headache that reaches its maximum intensity in less than 1 min and last about 5 minutes or more is:

a.) Migraine Headaches

b.) Post-Traumatic Headaches

c.) Cluster Headaches

d.) Thunderclap Headaches

357. In cold weather (below 2.5 to 0⁰c) when skin turns white and waxy or gray in color and mottled, but feels normal to touch. This condition known as:

a.) Frostnip

b.) Frostbite

c.) Cold stroke

d.) Cold bite

358. A condition in which skin and the tissue just below the skin freeze and hard to touch, is known as:

a.) Frostnip

b.) Frostbite

c.) Cold stroke

d.) Cold bite

359. Sledge Hammer Blow is seen in:

a.) Poisoning

b.) Lightning Flashes

c.) Asphyxia

d.) Firearm Injury

360. Cattle turking is seen in:

a.) Coronary Blood Vessels

b.) Retinal Blood Vessels

c.) Eye

d.) Liver

361. Abortion stick causes abortion by the mechanism of:

a.) Uterine contraction

b.) Placental Abruption

c.) Surgery

d.) All of the above

362. Two parallel linear bruises separated by an undamaged skin. This is following type of Bruise:

a.) Petechial Hemorrhages

b.) Tramline Bruises

c.) Intradermal Bruises

d.) Pad Bruises

363. Distinct Marking of the tire on the body are defined as::

a.) Petechial Hemorrhage

b.) Patterned Abrasion

c.) Pad Abrasion

d.) Contusion

364. Foamy liver is characteristic of:

a.) Adipocere

b.) Saponification

c.) Maceration

d.) Putrefaction

365. More than 5% carboxy-hemoglobin is measured in an non-smoker adult; death is due to:

a.) Arsenic Poisoning

b.) Antemortem Burns

c.) Methylene Chloride Poisoning

d.) b & c

366. Swelling of the scalp in a newborn is known as:

a.) Caput succedaneum

b.) Cephalhematoma

c.) Head Injury

d.) Cone Head

367. Septal Defect is also known as:

a.) Restricted blood flow

b.) Hole in the Heart

c.) Shortage of oxygen in body

d.) Electrical impulses in the heart

368. Atherosclerosis is a:

a.) Hardening and narrowing of arteries

b.) Hole in heart

c.) Restricted blood flow

d.) Shortage of oxygen in body

369. A group of many heart disease that are present at birth is known as:

a.) Atherosclerosis

b.) Septal defect

c.) Heart disease

d.) Cyanotic Heart Defect

370. Tachycardia is refers to:

a.) Fast blood flow

b.) Cardiac Arrest

c.) Fast Heart Rate

d.) Tache noire

371. Shearing damage is seen in:

a.) Brain

b.) Heart

c.) Uterus

d.) Gall bladder

372. Davidson body is used to determine:

a.) Age

b.) Race

c.) Sex

d.) Stature

373. Streak ovaries are seen in :

a.) Turner Syndrome

b.) Down Syndrome

c.) Klinfelter Syndrome

d.) Marfan's Syndrome

374. Cephalhematoma is a hemorrhage found between skull and periosteum in:

a.) An Adult

b.) A Child

c.) An old person aged about 60 and above

d.) A new born baby

375. Regarding human skull, which statement is correct:

a.) Frontal eminences are larger in females

b.) Occipital protuberances is more prominent in females

c.) Parietal eminences are larger in females

d.) a & c

376. True Hermaphroditism is when:

a.) Testes/ovaries are absent

b.) Testes and ovaries present in one individual

c.) Presence of Ovaries

d.) Presence of Testes

377. Krogman's formula is related to:

a.) Race

b.) Age

c.) Stature

d.) Sex

378. Best part for X-Ray to determine age of 7 years child:

a.) Iliac

b.) Wrist & Hand

c.) Pelvis

d.) Elbow

379. Palato print is commonly taken from which part of palate?

a.) Anterior Part

b.) Lateral wall

c.) Medial wall

d.) Posterior wall

380. Stature is determined by formula of:

a.) Locard's exchange principle

b.) Trotter and Gleser Formula

c.) Widmark Formula

d.) Hasse

381. Xenograft is transplantation of tissue:

a.) One part of body to another part of body

b.) From same species

c.) From different species

d.) All of the above

382. Under water autopsy of the heart is done in case of:

a.) Pneumothorax

b.) Air Embolism

c.) Myocardial Infraction

d.) Pulmonary Embolism

383. Hydrocution is:

a.) Immersion syndrome

b.) Hemolysis

c.) Dry drowning

d.) Wet drowning

384. The cause of death in immersion syndrome is:

a.) Ventricular Fibrillation

b.) Laryngeal Spasm

c.) Vagal Inhibition

d.) Asphyxia

385. Which one of the following is true about Immersion syndrome:

a.) Intense laryngeal spasm due to entry of water into nosopharynx a larynx.

b.) Due to sudden impact of the very cold water and causes death from cardiac arrest

c.) Circulatory Shock

d.) Water cross the alveolar membrane into the circulation

386. Fatal asphyxiation in child by putting food, toys into their mouth which obstruct the air passage is known as:

a.) Café coronary

b.) Crèche Coronary

c.) Gagging

d.) Choking

387. Tearing of the skin and tissue is known as:

a.) Laceration

b.) Contusion

c.) Abrasion

d.) Hemorrhage

388. Graze is a form of:

a.) Incised wound

b.) Abrasion

c.) Contusion

d.) Lacerated wound

389. Chop Wound is caused by following, except:

a.) Knife

b.) Tomahawk

c.) Axe

d.) Hatchet

390. Stab wounds are fatal when:

a.) Major pulmonary blood vessel has been cut

b.) Self-inflicted

c.) Penetration is about 1mm

d.) Stab in stomach

391. Perforating wound is:

a.) Weapons enter into the body producing only one wound.

b.) Weapons after entering into one side of the body will come out through the other side.

c.) Deep gaping wounds caused by a blow with the moderately sharp cutting edge of a heavy weapon.

d.) Incision is a clean cut wound through the tissue, caused by a sharp-edged instrument.

392. Injury is fabricated if:

a.) Location is easily reachable

b.) Multiple shallow, non-penetrating cuts or fingernail abrasions.

c.) Stab wound on chest

d.) a & b

393. Kronlein shot is a very rare injury of the skull caused by:

a.) Low-Velocity Bullet

b.) Medium-Velocity Bullet

c.) High-Velocity Bullet

d.) Any of the above

394. The distance of close shot is about:

a.) 1-1.5 cm from skin

b.) 10-20cm from skin

c.) 2.5-7.5 cm from skin

d.) 1 cm form skin

395. Bite mark is an example of:

a.) Scratch Abrasion

b.) Patterned Abrasion

c.) Imprint Abrasion

d.) Graze Abrasion

396. Bite marks can be found in case of:

a.) Rape

b.) Suicide

c.) Traffic accident

d.) Natural death

397. Blue color of contusion is due to:

a.) De-oxyhemoglobin

b.) Plasma

c.) Hematoidin

d.) Hemosiderin

398. Bruises seen on eyes, known as:

a.) Red Eye

b.) Black Eye

c.) Bruised Eye

d.) Swollen Eye

399. The bluish-black to brown discoloration of the bruise is due to:

a.) Hematoidin

b.) Bilirubin

c.) Hemosiderin

d.) Biliverdin

400. Green Color of contusion is due to:

a.) Biliverdin

b.) Hematoidin

c.) Hemosiderin

d.) Bilirubin

401. Antemortem bruise is differentiated from postmortem bruise by:

a.) Deoxyhemoglobin

b.) Hematoidin

c.) Capillary rupture with extravasation of blood

d.) Presence of little amount of blood

402. Split laceration looked like:

a.) Incised wound

b.) Contusion

c.) Abrasion

d.) burns

403. Hesitation cuts are seen in case of:

a.) Murder

b.) Suicide

c.) Accident

d.) Any of the above

404. Tissue bridges are seen in:

a.) Abrasion

b.) Contusion

c.) Laceration

d.) Stab wound

405. Incised wounds on genitalia:

a.) Homicidal

b.) Self-implicated

c.) Accidental

d.) Suicidal

406. Contact wound (made by firearm) shows:

a.) Abrasion collar

b.) Tattooing

c.) Cruciate splitting

d.) Burnt skin

407. Following are the feature of gunshot injury in skull, except:

a.) Entrance wound in beveled in the inner table

b.) Entrance wound beveled in the outer table

c.) Exit wound beveled in the outer table

d.) Exit wound beveled in the inner table

408. In firearm injury, there is boning, blackening, tattooing around the wound, and, is circular in shape; the injury is:

a.) Close shot entry

b.) Close contact exit

c.) Contact wound

d.) Distant shot

409. Molotov Cocktail is:

a.) Mixtures of alcohol

b.) Petrol Bombs

c.) A Special Drink

d.) A case of person named as Molotov

410. Which one is false about grievous hurt:

a.) Loss of one kidney

b.) Loss of hearing from one ear

c.) Fracture in hand

d.) Loss of one eye

411. Following increase the risk of bone fractures:

a.) Exercise

b.) Lack of sleep

c.) Tobacco and Nicotine

d.) Gender

412. How much blood is loss when the size of clot is of fist size:

a.) 10-50 ml

b.) 100-150 ml

c.) 200-300 ml

d.) 400-500 ml

413. Commonest cause of pulmonary embolism is:

a.) Fat

b.) Amniotic fluid

c.) Thrombus

d.) Air

414. What is the source of energy if person eat nothing since 7 days:

a.) Acetone

b.) Acetoacetate

c.) Glucose

d.) Amino acids

415. If person eat and drink nothing then he will die in:

a.) 1 week

b.) 2-5 days

c.) 2-3 week

d.) Few hours

416. Last one to disappear in starvation, is:

a.) Fat around abdomen

b.) Buccal fat

c.) Fat around the eyes

d.) Fat in the mesentery

417. In blast injury, most common organ affected:

a.) Eardrum

b.) Stomach

c.) Lungs

d.) Liver

418. Which of these factors influences healing of a wound?

a.) Diabetes

b.) Food

c.) Malnutrition

d.) a & c

419. Best prognostic indicator for head injured patients is:

a.) GCS (Glasgow Coma Scale)

b.) CT (Computerized Tomography) Scan

c.) History of patient

d.) Age

420. Antegrade amnesia is seen in:

a.) Post Traumatic Head Injury

b.) Drug Induced

c.) Electroconvulsive Therapy

d.) Stroke

421. Paradoxical undressing is seen in:

a.) Hyperthermia

b.) Hypothermia

c.) Tranvestism

d.) Immersion syndrome

422. Sweating is absent in:

a.) Immersion syndrome

b.) Heat stroke

c.) Heat cramps

d.) Hyperthermia

423. According to 'rule of 9', perineum burns constitute:

a.) 1%

b.) 25%

c.) 10%

d.) 50%

424. Heba classification is used for:

a.) Burn

b.) Age

c.) Stature

d.) Death

425. According to heba's classification burn are classified into:

a.) 1

b.) 2

c.) 3

d.) 4

426. Parkland formula is used for resuscitation of burns is for:

a.) Lactated Ringer's (LR)

b.) Normal Saline

c.) Glucose Saline

d.) 25% Dextrose

427. Muils and Barclays formula is for:

a.) Anthropometry

b.) Stature

c.) Colloid based resuscitation in major burns

d.) Sex determination

428. In the case of burning, blister burst after:

a.) 2-3 days

b.) 5-6 days

c.) 8-10 days

d.) 11-12 days

429. Blister Formation occurred in burn after:

a.) 1 hour

b.) 2 hour

c.) 3 hour

d.) 4 hour

430. Primary impact injury must commonly seen in :

a.) Head

b.) Throax

c.) Eyes

d.) Abdomen

431. Most common organ injured in penetrating injury of the abdomen:

a.) Liver

b.) Spleen

c.) Stomach

d.) Small intestine

432. Someone else's fertilized egg is implanted in another woman, this is known as:

a.) Traditional Surrogacy

b.) Gestational Surrogacy

c.) Primary Surrogacy

d.) All of the above

433. Atavism is inheritance of feature of:

a.) Father

b.) Grandmother

c.) Mother

d.) Brother

434. Hymen can be rupture by all; except:

a.) Sexual intercourse

b.) Surgical operation

c.) Sanitary Tampons

d.) Exercise

435. The Common Site and Traumatic rupture of hymen is seen on the:

a.) Anterior Aspect

b.) Posterior Aspect

c.) Lateral Aspect

d.) Posterio-Lateral Aspect

436. In following situation Hymen may not rupture after rape:

a.) Penetration was not full

b.) Hymen is tough, fleshy and elastic

c.) In deflorated women

d.) All of the above

437. Most common cause of erectile dysfunction:

a.) Psychological

b.) Drug induced

c.) Alcohol

d.) Diabetes

438. Test for vaginal cells in case of rape is:

a.) Alternate light source

b.) Acid phosphatase test

c.) Lugol's Iodine

d.) Benzidine Test

439. In Algolagnia:

a.) Person gets sexual gratification by infliction of pain or physical cruelty.

b.) The person gets sexual gratification by inducing his wife to have sexual intercourse with another man.

c.) Person gets sexual gratification by collecting opposite sex clothes.

d.) Person wears opposite sex clothes to get sexual gratification.

440. Lust murder is an extreme form of:

a.) Troilism

b.) Masochism

c.) Algolagnia

d.) Lesbianism

441. Buccal Coitus is related to:

a.) Oral Intercourse

b.) Anal Intercourse

c.) Sexual Intercourse

d.) Rape

442. No spermatozoa recovered from semen, in case of:

a.) Azoospermia

b.) Vasectomy

c.) Old age

d.) All of the above

443. The stains on the clothes can be identified conclusively as semen by :

a.) Acid Phosphatase Test

b.) Barberio's Test

c.) Spermatozoa

d.) All Of the Above

444. 'Falanga' is:

a.) Electric current for torture

b.) Pulling of hair

c.) Hitting the feet with stick

d.) Self-inflicted injury

445. Which body fluid is not responsible for the transmission of HIV:

a.) Semen

b.) Breast Milk

c.) Tears

d.) Blood

446. HLA typing is useful in:

a.) Disputed paternity

b.) Organ transplant

c.) a & b

d.) Dactylography

447. The term "Halitosis" denotes which one of the following:

a.) Hearing Impairment

b.) Vision Impairment

c.) Bad Breath

d.) Excessive Sweating

448. Disease of which among the following are included in degenerative disease?

a.) Heart

b.) Joint

c.) Nervous system

d.) All of the above

449. Antibiotics in high dose can cause the suppression of synthesis of which one of the following vitamins in human body?

a.) Vitamin A

b.) Biotin

c.) Vitamin K

d.) Vitamin B

450. Bowman's Glands are located in the:

a.) Anterior pituitary

b.) Olfactory epithelium of our nose

c.) Proximal end or uriniferous tubules

d.) In hand

451. Human RBC placed in 1.5% NaCl solution will:

a.) Burst

b.) Shrink

c.) No effect

d.) Extended

452. When blood of one individual is mixed with another individual's blood/serum, clotting of RBC may occur because of:

a.) Antigen-Antibody Reaction

b.) Antibody-Antibody Reaction

c.) Antigen-Antigen Reaction

d.) None of the above

453. Progesterone is secreted by:

a.) Thymus

b.) Thyroid

c.) Testis

d.) Corpus luteum

454. Injury of which of these nerve cause vocal cord paralysis?

a.) External Laryngeal

b.) Recurrent Laryngeal

c.) Internal Laryngeal

d.) Superior Laryngeal

455. In deltoid paralysis, which nerve is involve:

a.) Musculocutaneous Nerve

b.) Circumflex Nerve

c.) Radial Nerve

d.) Axillary Nerve

456. Lockwood ligament is found in:

a.) Temporomandibular Joint (TMJ)

b.) Pharynx

c.) Larynx

d.) Orbit

457. What if ligament is torn?

a.) Bones will move freely at joint

b.) Bones will never be fixed

c.) Bones will fix automatically

d.) Bone less movable at joint and will pain

458. The end of long bones contains following cartilage:

a.) Calcified cartilage

b.) Hyaline Cartilage

c.) Fibrous Cartilage

d.) Elastic Cartilage

459. Kuffer's cells occur in:

a.) Liver

b.) Kidney

c.) Spleen

d.) Brain

460. Following part of the body secrets the hormone secretin:

a.) Ileum

b.) Rectum

c.) Duodenum

d.) Esophagus

461. Which one of the following is the type of joint between the skull bones of human:

a.) Cartilaginous Joint

b.) Hinge Joint

c.) Fibrous Joint

d.) Synovial Joint

462. Which of the following may be used to estimate the age of person at time of his/her death with regard to skeletonized human remains:

a.) Adipocere formation

b.) Superimposition

c.) Epiphyseal union

d.) Hypostasis

463. Fingernails are made up of:

a.) Potassium

b.) Calcium

c.) Keratin

d.) Sodium

464. Northern blot test is used for:

a.) DNA Analysis

b.) RNA Analysis

c.) Protein Analysis

d.) Enzyme Analysis

465. Telefona is:

a.) Beating on both ears

b.) Beating on back

c.) Beating on soles

d.) Beating on hands

466. A person found dead in his room. He was hanged by rope from sealing fan. Body has Dribbling of saliva, noncontinuous ligature mark and dilated eyes. His fists were clenched. This is case of:

a.) Suicide

b.) Homicide

c.) Accidental

d.) Lynching

467. If a dead body of human is floating on the surface of river in month of May. The person has been dead from:

a.) 1 days

b.) 2-3 days

c.) 1-2 weeks

d.) 15-20 days

468. Jaundice is caused by:

a.) Excessive collection of Calcium in body

b.) Excessive Protein in the body

c.) Excessive level of Vitamins in body

d.) Excessive level of Bilirubin in the body

469. Maximum drugs are metabolized in:

a.) Kidney

b.) Brain

c.) Small Intestine

d.) Liver

470. Movement of food in intestine and circular muscle in the stomach is:

a.) Digestion

b.) Peristalsis

c.) Active motion

d.) Constipation

471. If food is found in the small intestine, but stomach is empty then death occurred:

a.) 1-2 hours after meal

b.) 10-12 hours after meal

c.) 4-6 hours after meal

d.) Few minutes after meal

472. Tonsil is a:

a.) Muscular Tissue

b.) Lymphoid Tissue

c.) Connective Tissue

d.) Epithelial Tissue

473. Diuretics causes loss of:

a.) Sodium

b.) Potassium

c.) Calcium

d.) Iron

474. A child teeth stained permanently after exposure from:

a.) Diphenyl Hydantoin

b.) Diphenhydramine

c.) Digoxin

d.) Doxycycline

475. According to Dupuytren's classification blister formation is graded as:

a.) I Degree

b.) II Degree

c.) III Degree

d.) IV Degree

476. The identification of dead body can be done by:

a.) Putrefied body

b.) Place of Occurrence

c.) Laundry & Tailor marks on cloths

d.) None

477. The situation in which the blood separates into distinct units is known as:

a.) Ophthalmologic Changes

b.) Trucking

c.) Dilation

d.) Contraction

478. Which insects are the first to appear on the dead body:

a.) Beetles

b.) Ants

c.) Flies

d.) Mites

479. In which stage house-flies begin to appear and deposit eggs:

a.) Fresh Stage

b.) Post-Decay Stage

c.) Bloated Stage

d.) Decay Stage

480. Corpse appears normal on the outside, but is starting to decompose and insects starts laying eggs:

a.) Fresh Stage

b.) Active Decay Stage

c.) Post Decay Stage

d.) Decay Stage

481. Which stage begins with the splitting of the skin to allow the gases to escape?

a.) Rigor Mortis

b.) Decay Stage

c.) Bloated Stage

d.) Post-decay Stage

482. Which stage occurs due to activity of bacteria which produce gases inside the body?

a.) Rigor Mortis

b.) Decay Stage

c.) Bloated Stage

d.) Post-decay Stage

483. Cyanosis occurs when the concentration of reduced hemoglobin exceeds:

a.) 10 gm %

b.) 5 gm%

c.) 15 gm%

d.) 2 gm%

484. Cyanosis commonly known as:

a.) Oxygenated disease

b.) Decreased hemoglobin

c.) Blue hands or feet

d.) Cyan

485. Cyanosis is caused by:

a.) An increased concentration of reduced hemoglobin

b.) A decreased concentration of oxyhemoglobin

c.) Hypoxia

d.) A decreased concentration of hemoglobin

486. Commonest cause of hemobilia is:

a.) Gall stones

b.) Trauma

c.) Cholangitis

d.) Hepatoma

487. In India, Splenectomy is most commonly performed for:

a.) Hydatid cyst

b.) Carcinoma thyroid

c.) Trauma

d.) Portal hypertension

488. Larvae are voracious feeders in following stage of the fly cycle:

a.) Ist Instar

b.) IInd Instar

c.) IIIrd Instar

d.) IVth Instar

489. If larvae are found in stage IInd and IIIrd then person has been dead from:

a.) 2-4 days

b.) 8-10 days

c.) 10-14 days

d.) 2 Weeks

Forensic Medicine

490. Following blowflies don't have much forensic value, as it is unclear whether they have just arrived at the scene or have developed on the body:

a.) Adult

b.) Juvenile

c.) Larvae

d.) Pupae

491. Rule of Thumb determines:

a.) Height

b.) Length of wound

c.) Postmortem Estimation

d.) Fingerprints

492. Formula of Rule Of Thumb:

a.) Stature x PMI/48

b.) Heat Loss = 1ºC per hour

c.) Temperature of body x TOD/24

d.) Stature =PMI/48

493. Glaister equation:

a.) Calculates the structure of bone

b.) Calculates the hours passing after death

c.) Calculates the stature

d.) Calculates the total fractures in body

494. Glaister equation is:

a.) 98.7°F - Rectal Temperature /1.5°C per hour = PMI

b.) 98.7°F – the dead body temperature

c.) 98.7°F/1.5°C per hour

d.) Rectal temperature/1.5°C per hour

495. In antemortem tooth loss or extraction, the alveolus is:

a.) Smooth

b.) Sharp and feathered

c.) Does not show any injury

d.) May have a regular appearance

496. Infanticide is:

a.) Killing of child aged about 11-15 year

b.) Killing of child

c.) Killing of newly born child within one year

d.) Killing of 0-5 year old child

497. How many bones are in the skeleton of an infant?

a.) 206

b.) 300

c.) Skeleton are made up of cartilage

d.) 250

498. Direct impact on bone may produce

a.) Spiral fracture

b.) Transverse fracture

c.) Oblique fracture

d.) Avulsion fracture

499. The body digest food within:

a.) 5-10 hours

b.) 7-8 hours

c.) 10-12 hours

d.) 24-72 hours

500. Othello syndrome related to:

a.) Person feels that his/her partner has been disloyal.

b.) Person believes that everyone, every matter concerning him/her.

c.) He/she belief that he is suffering from dangerous disease.

d.) Person does not believe in his/her existence.

Answer-Sheet

Forensic Medicine

1	a	2	c	3	b	4	b	5	a
6	c	7	b	8	a	9	e	10	b
11	d	12	a	13	c	14	c	15	a
16	c	17	d	18	b	19	d	20	b
21	b	22	d	23	c	24	c	25	d
26	b	27	d	28	a	29	c	30	a
31	a	32	b	33	d	34	d	35	c
36	c	37	c	38	a	39	a	40	b
41	c	42	b	43	a	44	c	45	d
46	a	47	b	48	a	49	b	50	a
51	d	52	a	53	d	54	a	55	b
56	a	57	d	58	a	59	c	60	d
61	b	62	c	63	b	64	c	65	a
66	d	67	d	68	a	69	b	70	b
71	a	72	b	73	a	74	c	75	a
76	d	77	d	78	c	79	c	80	c
81	a	82	b	83	c	84	a	85	b
86	b	87	b	88	a	89	c	90	c
91	a	92	d	93	c	94	c	95	d
96	d	97	c	98	d	99	c	100	c

101	b	102	d	103	b	104	d	105	b
106	c	107	a	108	c	109	a	110	d
111	b	112	d	113	d	114	b	115	d
116	b	117	b	118	b	119	d	120	d
121	b	122	c	123	c	124	d	125	b
126	a	127	b	128	d	129	c	130	a
131	b	132	a	133	b	134	b	135	b
136	d	137	a	138	a	139	b	140	a
141	d	142	a	143	b	144	d	145	c
146	a	147	a	148	b	149	a	150	c
151	b	152	d	153	b	154	c	155	d
156	b	157	a	158	b	159	c	160	c
161	b	162	d	163	a	164	a	165	a
166	c	167	a	168	b	169	d	170	b
171	a	172	c	173	b	174	c	175	c
176	c	177	a	178	d	179	a	180	d
181	d	182	c	183	c	184	b	185	a
186	c	187	a	188	b	189	a	190	b
191	c	192	c	193	c	194	b	195	d
196	a	197	b	198	c	199	d	200	a

201	b	202	b	203	a	204	a	205	b
206	c	207	a	208	d	209	a	210	d
211	c	212	d	213	c	214	a	215	a
216	a	217	a	218	b	219	c	220	d
221	a	222	b	223	b	224	a	225	a
226	e	227	b	228	d	229	a	230	b
231	b	232	b	233	b	234	d	235	a
236	c	237	c	238	d	239	c	240	c
241	b	242	a	243	b	244	b	245	a
246	b	247	c	248	a	249	b	250	b
251	c	252	e	253	b	254	a	255	c
256	b	257	b	258	a	259	d	260	b
261	c	262	d	263	c	264	d	265	b
266	a	267	a	268	b	269	a	270	b
271	a	272	b	273	c	274	d	275	b
276	c	277	d	278	c	279	d	280	d
281	b	282	d	283	c	284	a	285	a
286	b	287	d	288	c	289	a	290	a
291	c	292	d	293	b	294	b	295	c
296	a	297	b	298	c	299	d	300	b

301	b	302	b	303	c	304	c	305	b
306	d	307	b	308	a	309	b	310	c
311	d	312	a	313	d	314	b	315	c
316	d	317	b	318	c	319	d	320	a
321	d	322	b	323	e	324	a	325	a
326	b	327	b	328	a	329	d	330	c
331	a	332	c	333	a	334	b	335	d
336	b	337	a	338	b	339	e	340	c
341	a	342	a	343	b	344	d	345	b
346	c	347	d	348	a	349	a	350	c
351	b	352	c	353	c	354	c	355	b
356	d	357	a	358	b	359	b	360	b
361	a	362	b	363	b	364	d	365	d
366	a	367	b	368	a	369	d	370	c
371	a	372	c	373	a	374	d	375	d
376	b	377	d	378	b	379	a	380	b
381	c	382	b	383	a	384	c	385	b
386	b	387	a	388	b	389	a	390	a
391	a	392	d	393	c	394	c	395	b
396	a	397	a	398	b	399	c	400	a

401	c	402	a	403	b	404	c	405	a
406	c	407	b	408	a	409	b	410	c
411	c	412	d	413	c	414	a	415	c
416	b	417	a	418	d	419	a	420	a
421	b	422	c	423	a	424	a	425	d
426	a	427	c	428	b	429	a	430	c
431	a	432	b	433	b	434	d	435	d
436	d	437	a	438	c	439	a	440	c
441	a	442	d	443	d	444	c	445	c
446	c	447	c	448	d	449	b	450	b
451	b	452	a	453	d	454	b	455	d
456	d	457	d	458	b	459	a	460	c
461	c	462	c	463	c	464	b	465	a
466	a	467	b	468	d	469	d	470	b
471	c	472	b	473	b	474	d	475	b
476	c	477	b	478	c	479	d	480	a
481	b	482	c	483	b	484	c	485	d
486	b	487	c	488	c	489	a	490	a
491	c	492	b	493	b	494	a	495	b
496	c	497	b	498	b	499	d	500	a

BIBLIOGRAPHY AND SUGGESTED READING

- Some questions have been taken from different competitive examinations question papers.

- The Merck Veterinary Manual (2016). Chapter "Herbicide Poisoning" by PK GUPTA 11th edition, Merck & Co. Inc Whitehouse Station, NJ, USA 2969-99

- *Textbook of Forensic Medicine and Toxicology, V. V. Pillay, 14th edition, p369.*

- Gupta PK (2016) Essential Concepts in Toxicology. Published by PharmaMed Press (A unit of BSP Books Pvt. Ltd), Hyderabad, India pp 362

- Anderson, M. E., R. S. Thomas, K. W. Gaido, et al. Dose - response modeling in reproductive toxicology in the systems biology era. *Reprod. Toxicol.* 19 : 327 – 337, 2005.

- Deighton, N. Metabolomics. In *Molecular and Biochemical Toxicology,* eds. R. C. Smart and E. Hodgson, pp. 67 – 79. Hoboken, NJ: Wiley, 2008.

- Edwards, S. W. and R. J. Preston. Systems biology and mode of action based risk assessment. *Toxically. Sci.* 106: 312 – 318, 2008.

- Harrill, A. H., P. K. Ross, D. M. Gatti, et al. Population - based discovery of toxicogenomics biomarkers for hepatotoxicity using a laboratory strain diversity panel. *Toxicol.Sci.* 110: 235 – 243, 2009.

- Merrick, B. A. Proteomics. In *Molecular and Biochemical Toxicology,* eds. R. C. Smart and E. Hodgson, pp. 41 – 66. Hoboken, NJ: Wiley, 2008.

- National Research Council. Toxicity testing in the 21st century: A vision and a strategy.

- Washington, DC: National Research Council Committee on Toxicity Testing and Assessment of Environmental Agents, National Academy Press, 2007.

- Olelsiak, M. F. Toxicogenomics. In *Molecular and Biochemical Toxicology,* eds. R. C. Smart and E. Hodgson, pp. 25 – 39. Hoboken, NJ: Wiley, 2008.

- Plant, N. Can systems toxicology identify common biomarkers of non - genotoxic carcinogenesis? *Toxicology* 254: 164 – 169, 2008.

- Smart, R. C. and E. Hodgson, eds. *Molecular and Biochemical Toxicology.* Hoboken, NJ: John Wiley and Sons, 2008.

- Stone, E. A. and D. M. Nielsen. Bioinformatics. In *Molecular and Biochemical Toxicology,* eds.

- R. C. Smart and E. Hodgson, pp. 81 – 107. Hoboken, NJ: Wiley, 2008.

- Waring, J. F., R. Ciurlionis, R. A. Jolly, et al. Microarray analysis of hepatotoxins in vitro reveals a correlation between gene expression profile les and mechanisms of toxicity. *Toxicol.Lett.* 120: 359 – 368, 2001.

- Joy, R. M. Neurotoxicology: Central and peripheral. In *Encyclopedia of Toxicology*, vol. 2,P. Wexler, ed. New York: Academic Press, 1998, pp. 389–413.

- Stryer, L. *Biochemistry*, 4th ed. San Francisco: W. H. Freeman, 1999.

- Eaton, D. L., and C. D. Klaassen. Principles of toxicology In *Casarrett and Doull's Toxicology: The Basic Science of Poisons*, 6th ed. C. D. Klaassen, ed. New York: McGraw-Hill, 2001, pp.11–34.

- Calabrese, E. J., and L. A. Baldwin. U-shaped dose-responses in biology, toxicology, and publichealth. *An. Rev. Public Health* 22: 15–33, 2001.

- Bondar, V. S. Toxicological chemistry. Schemes and Tables: Handbook for students of higher schools / V. S. Bondar, S. A. Karpushina. – Kharkiv: NUPh: Golden Pages, 2009. – 120 p.

- Karpushina, S. A. Toxicological chemistry. Lecture course / S. A. Karpushina, V. S. Bondar, I. A. Zhuravel. – Kharkiv: NUPh: Golden pages, 2011. – 208 p.

- Toxicological Chemistry. Laboratory workbook / S. A. Karpushina, I. A. Zhuravel, V. S. Bondar, S. V. Bayurka. – Kharkiv: NUPh, 2012. – 63 p.

- Baselt, C. R. Disposition of Toxic Drugs and Chemicals in Man: 9-th edition / R. C. Baselt. – California: Biomedical Publications, 2011. – 1900 p.

- Basic Analytical Toxicology / R. J. Flanagan [et al.]. – Geneva: World Health organization, 1995. – 363 p.

- Bell, S. Forensic Chemistry / S. Bell. – New Jersey: Pearson Prentice Hall. – 671 p.

- Clarke's analysis of drugs and poisons in pharmaceuticals, body fluids and postmortem material: 4-th edition / A. C. Moffat [et al.]. – London; Chicago: Pharmaceutical Press, 2011. – 2736 p.

- Clarke's Analytical Forensic Toxicology / ed. by Sue Jickells, Adam Negrusz. – London: Pharmaceutical Press, 2008. – 648 p.

- Flanagan, R. J. Developing Analytical Toxicology Services: Principles and Guidance [Electronic resource] / R. J. Flanagan. – Geneva: World Health Organization, 2005. – 36 p. – Available at: http://www.who.int/ipcs/publications/training_poisons/hospitalnalyti cal_toxicology.pdf (date of the application: (07.09.2017). – Developing Analytical Toxicology Services: Principles and Guidance.

- Gracia RC, Snodgrass WR. Lead toxicity and chelation therapy. Am J Health Syst Pharm. 2007 Jan 1; 64(1):45-53.

- Mann KV, Travers JD. Succimer, an oral lead chelator. Clin Pharm. 1991 Dec; 10(12):914-22.

- Patrick L. Lead toxicity, a review of the literature. Part 1: Exposure, evaluation, and treatment. Altern Med Rev. 2006 Mar; 11(1):2-22.

- Poisoning & Drug Overdose. Fourth Edition / ed. by Kent R. Olson. – Zange Medical Books, Mc Graw-Hill, 2004. – 718 p.

- https://en.wikipedia.org/wiki/History_of_poison.

- Kaviraja Ambikadutta Shastri: Editor, Susrutsamhita of Maharsi-Susruta Edited with AyurvedaTatva-Sandipika, Kalpasthana; Sthavarvish-vidnyaniyam Adhyaya: Chapter 2, Verse 33, Chaukhmba Sanskrit Sansthan Publication, Varanasi, Second Edition, part 1, 2010; 32 [45]

- Udayvir Shastri: Editor, Kautilaya Arthashasrta of Vishnugupta Kautalya Edited with 'Nayachandrika' Hindi Commentry, Volume 2, Ashumrutak Parikshan,Chapter no. 82, Verse 21-30.Bharat Bharti publication, Delhi, Second Edition.1969:135-137.

- https://en.wikipedia.org/wiki/History_of_poison.

- Dr. Parikh C.K., Parikh's Textbook of Medical Jourisprudence Forensic Medicine and Toxicology, Section VIII, Introduction to Toxicology, CBS Publishers & Distributors, Dehli, Sixth Edition Reprint-2007; 8(9).

- Dr. Mathiharan K, Dr. Patnaik AK.Modi's Medical Jurisprudence and Toxicology, Section 2,Diagnosis of Poisoning:Chapter 1,Lexis Nexis Publication, Dehli,Twenty Third Edition, 2006: 21-29

- Dr. U. R. Shekhar Namburi, editor. Agadtantra, Diagnosis of Poisoning, Chapter 05, 1st edition, Chaukhambha Sanskrit Sansthan Varanasi, 2013; 41 & 42.

- Dr. Brahmanand Tripathi, Editor, Charakasamhita of Agnivesha Edited with 'Charak-Chandrika' Hindi Commentary, Volume 2, Chikitsasthana;

Vishachikitsaadhyaya, Chapter 23, verse 16, Chaukhmba Surbharati Prakashan, Delhi, Reprint, 2002; 749.

- Kaviraja Ambikadutta Shastri: Editor, Susrutsamhita of Maharsi-Susruta Edited with AyurvedaTatva-Sandipika, Kalpasthana; Sthavarvishvidnyaniyam Adhyaya: Chapter 1, Verse 42, Chaukhmba Sanskrit Sansthan Publication, Varanasi, Second Edition, part 1, 2010; 08.

- Prof. K. R. Srikant Murthy, editor Ashtanga Sangraha of Vagbhata, Sutrasthana, Annaraksha Vidhi Adhyaya, 8/48, 9th edition, Chaukhmbha Orientalia, Varanasi, 2005; 167.

- Kaviraja Ambikadutta Shastri: Editor, Susrutsamhita of Maharsi-Susruta Edited with AyurvedaTatva-Sandipika, Kalpasthana; Sthavarvishvidnyaniyam Adhyaya: Chapter 1, Verse 56, Chaukhmba Sanskrit Sansthan Publication, Varanasi, Second Edition, part 1, 2010; 11.

- Dr. Brahmanand Tripathi: Editor, Ashtanghrudayam of Shrimadvagbhata Edited with 'Nirmala Hindi commentary', Uttarasthan; Vishpratishedhadhyay, Chapter 35, Verse, 50-53, Chaukhmba Sanskrit Pratishthan, Delhi: Reprint, 2007; 1150.

- Udayvir Shastri: Editor, Kautilaya Arthashasrta of Vishnugupta Kautalya Edited with 'Nayachandrika' Hindi Commentry, Volume 2, Ashumrutak Parikshan, Chapter no. 82. Bharat Bharti publication, Delhi, Second Edition, 1969; 135-137.

- Dr. Parikh C.K., Parikh's Textbook of Medical Jourisprudence Forensic Medicine and Toxicology, Section 10, Fuels, 52, CBS Publishers & Distributors, Dehli, Sixth Edition Reprint-2007; 10.39.

- Bardale Rajesh, Principles of Forensic Medicine and Toxicology, Section 2, Toxicology:General Considerations:Chapter 33,The Health Science Publishers,Dehli,,Second Editon, 2017; 473-474.

- Dr. Parikh C.K., Parikh's Textbook of Medical Jourisprudence Forensic Medicine and Toxicology,Section VIII, Introduction to Toxicology, CBS Publishers & Distributors, Dehli, Sixth Edition Reprint-2007; 8.11.

- AK Jaiswal, Handbook of Forensic Analytical Toxicology, chapter no.4, Thin Layer Chromatography and its application, 1st edition, Jaypee publication Dehli, 2014; 139.

- http://plato.mercyhurst.edu/chemistry/kjircitano/ChemPrincLaboratories/Drugs.

- AK Jaiswal, Handbook of Forensic Analytical Toxicology, chapter no.5, Thin Layer Chromatography and its application, 1st edition, Jaypee publication Dehli, 2014; 214.

- Dr. Mathiharan K, Dr. Patnaik AK.Modi's Medical Jurisprudence and Toxicology, Section 2, Poisons and their Medicolegal Aspects: Chapter 1,Lexis Nexis Publication, Dehli,Twenty Third Edition, 2006; 29.

- https://www.eolss.net/Sample-Chapters/C09/E6-12-23-00.pdf.

- Blanke RV, Poklis A, Analytic/Forensic Toxicology In: Amdur MO, Doull J, Klaassen CD editors. Cascarett and Doull's Toxicology The Basic Science of Poisons.4th ed. London: Pergamon Press, 1992; 905-923.

- 54. Dr. Mathiharan K, Dr. Patnaik AK., Modi's Medical Jurisprudence and Toxicology, Section 2, Poisons and their Medicolegal Aspects: Chapter 1,Lexis Nexis Publication, Dehli, Twenty Third Edition, 2006; 29.

- http://plato.mercyhurst.edu/chemistry/kjircitano/ChemPrincLaboratories/Drugs.

- AK Jaiswal, Handbook of Forensic Analytical Toxicology, chapter no.12, Breath Alcohol Analyser and its application, 1st edition, Jaypee publication Dehli, 2014; 442-444.

- Broughton, P. M. G. A rapid ultraviolet spectrophotometric method for the detection, estimation and identification of barbiturates in biological material.

- *Biochem. J.* 63 (1956) 207.

- Clarke, E. G. C. (Ed.) *Isolation and Identification 0/ Drugs*(1969) Pharmaceutical Press, London, £14.00.

- Curry. A. S. *Simple Tests to Detect Poisoning. (1966)* Association of Clinical Pathologists Broadsheet No. 52,25p.

- Curry, A. S. *Poison Detection in Human Organs.* 2nd ed.(1969) Thomas, Springfield, £5.78.

- Dauphinais, R. M., McComb, R. A specific procedure for serum glutethimide (Doriden) determination. *Amer.J. Cl/in. Path.* 44 (1965) 440.

- Forrest, I. S., Forrest, F. M., Mason, A. S. A rapid urine colour test for imipramine (TofraniI, Geigy): supplementary report with colour chart. *Amer. J. Psychiat.* 116 (1960) 1021.

- Forrest, I. S., Forrest, F. M. Urine colour test for the detection of phenothiazine compounds. *Clin. Chem.* 6 (1960) 11.

- Garvey, K., Bowden, C. M. The colorimetric determination of barbiturates. *Proc. Assoc. clin. Biochem.* 4 (1966) 20.

- Lawson, A. A. H., Brown, S. S. Acute methaqualone (Mandrax) poisoning. *Scot. med. J-.* 12 (1967) 63.

- Matthew, H., Lawson, A. A. H. *Treatment 0f Common Acute Poisonings.* 2nd ed. (1970), Livingstone, Edinburgh, £1.00.

- Routh, J. I., Shane, N. A., Arredondo, E. G., Paul, W. D. Determination of N-acetyl-p-aminophtnol in plasma. *Clin. Chem.* 14 (1968) 882.

- Sunshine, I. *Handbook 0f Analytical Toxicology. (1969)* Chemical Rubber Co., Cleveland, £14'00.

- Sunshine, I., Gerber, S. R. *Spectrophotometric Analysis 0f Drugs.* Including Atlas of Spectra (1963) Thomas, Springfield, £4.50.

- Todd, R. G. (Ed.) *Extra Pharmacopoeia: Martindale,* 25th ed. (1967) Pharmaceutical Press, London, £7.50.

- Trinder, P. Rapid determination of salicylate in biological fluids. *Biochem. J.* 57 (1954) 301.

- Whitehead, T. P., Worthington, S. The determination of carboxyhaemoglobin. *Clin. chim. Acta* 6 (1961) 356.

- Kanji S, MacLean RD. Cardiac glycoside toxicity: more than 200 years and counting. Crit Care Clin. 2012 Oct; 28(4):527-35.

- Smith TW. Digitalis. Mechanisms of action and clinical use. N Engl J Med. 1988 Feb 11; 318(6):358-65.

- Wright RO et al. Methemoglobinemia: etiology, pharmacology, and clinical management. Ann Emerg Med. 1999 Nov;34(5):646-56.

- Schillinger BM et al. Boric Acid Poisoning. J Am Acad Dermatol. 1982 Nov;7(5):667-73.

- Piantadosi CA. Carbon monoxide poisoning. N Engl J Med. 2002 Oct 3;347(14):1054-5.

- Mazzone A, Dal Canton A. Image in clinical medicine. Hypercarotenemia. N Engl J Med. 2002 Mar 14;346(11):821.

- Hochholzer W. The facts behind niacin. Ther Adv Cardiovasc Dis. 2011 Oct;5(5):227-40.

www.ingramcontent.com/pod-product-compliance
Lightning Source LLC
Chambersburg PA
CBHW060843220526
45466CB00003B/1226